CROW MERCIES

By Penelope Scambly Schott

Sarah Lantz Memorial Poetry Book Prize Award

Final Judge—Colleen J. McElroy

CALYX Books
Corvallis, Oregon

Publication of this book is supported in part by Eleanor Wilner and Robert Weinberg, whose donation established the Sarah Lantz Memorial Poetry Prize; by grants from the Kinsman Foundation and the Spirit Mountain Community Fund; and by the generous support of Sara Burant and Gene Johnson and Mary Alice Seville.

Cover art "The Visitors" by William E. Shumway
Cover and book design by Cheryl McLean

CALYX Books are distributed to the trade through Consortium Book Sales and Distribution, Inc., 1-800-283-3572. CALYX Books are also available through major library distributors, jobbers, and most small press distributors including Baker & Taylor, Ingram, and Small Press Distribution. For personal orders or other information: CALYX Books, PO Box B, Corvallis, OR 97339, (541) 753-9384, FAX (541) 753-0515, www.calyxpress.org

∞

The paper in this book meets the guidelines for permanence and durability of the Committee on Production Guidelines for Book Longevity of the Council on Library Resources and the minimum requirements of the American National Standard for the Permanence of Paper for Printed Library Materials Z38.48-1984.

Library of Congress Cataloging-in-Publication Data
Schott, Penelope Scambly
        Crow Mercies / by Penelope Scambly Schott

p. cm.
ISBN 978-0-934971-11-9 (pbk. : alk. paper) : $14.95.
I. Title.

PS3569.C5283C76 2010
811'.54—dc22

                                        2010007252

Printed in the U.S.A.
9 8 7 6 5 4 3 2 1

In memory of Sarah Lantz
and all my other poet sisters
who died too soon

ACKNOWLEDGMENTS

Anderbo: "Fugitive Memory"; *Cloudbank:* "A Long Ago Summer Where I First Existed as Who I Would Become"; *Compass Rose:* "Fugitive Memory"; *Damselfly Press:* "Dear Lady"; *Dos Passos Review:* "Thin Places"; *Fieralingue:* "Biopsy," "U.S. Air Force Admits It May Have Bombed Civilians in Afghanistan"; *Front Range:* "Why I Must Build a Fence," "My Dead Mother as a Calypso Orchid"; *Inspirit:* "Like Any Other Child" (2nd prize); *Kaleidoscope:* "Calling My Mother Again"; *National League of American Pen Women:* "The Geology of My Grandparents' House" (2nd prize), "Sweet Emma" (honorable mention); *Natural Bridge:* "Morpho," "Autobiography III: My Disenchanted Life"; *Smartish Pace:* "Holes in the World" (finalist in Beullah Rose contest); *Sweet:* "Here's How I Used to Make Myself Cry," "There Once Was a Horse Who Loved His Bells"; *Switched On Gutenberg:* "Communications at Sea"; *Thresholds:* "Biopsy," "Prayer" (section 18 from *"Fun Tonight!* A Composition in Eighteen Fragments"), "A Stone Wrote a Song"; *US 1 Worksheets,* "At Santiago de Atitlán"; *Verseweavers,* "Because the Earth Is Slowing Down" (1st prize); *VoiceCatcher5:* "Reclining Nude"; *Windfall,* "Memorial"; *Xanadu,* "Because the Earth Is Slowing Down"

CONTENTS

I

II

III

MORPHO

I want to meet the man who named the butterflies:
    the *Morpho patroclus,*
    the *Graphium agamemnon* with neon spots,
    the famous *Papilio ulysses* who feeds on lantana
    and is lured by the waving of blue cloth.

Or else it was a woman who chose those names,
a woman alone each night in her tent,
no man but Homer
safe to take to bed.
Yes, I'm sure it was a woman.

When I find this woman in her lilac smock,
I will uncork a bottle of nectar. We will drink
to the tipsy banded *Morpho patroclus*
who wobbles in air from fermented fruit.
She and I will sip from the same chipped cup

knowing we both know how to be patient,
knowing how Helen on the walls of Troy
lifted her breasts like brilliant high fruit,
and how our own stretch marks and scars
turn iridescent along the ancient trade routes.

PENELOPE TO HER HUSBAND,
OR WHY I SOMETIMES NEED TO VOYAGE WITHOUT YOU

Because you look so handsome
in your washed gray shirt

Because our bedstead is hewn
from black oak

Because the dog watches me
whenever I move

Because coyotes yip
past the end of our dead end street,

and as I stare through this bottle of Greek olive oil,
the horizon glows citron green

Because years fall down behind me
like discarded clothing

Wherever I go, I bring the world home
in the palms of my hands,

and you eat

ABOVE THE LITTLE NORTH SANTIAM RIVER

– for my mother

When I walk through the tall forest,
trees gather behind me.
They whisper my cold name
which isn't Bunchberry or Slippery Jack
or Good Daughter or even Penelope,
which certainly isn't human.

When I walk in the deep forest,
a barred owl follows my shadow,
hunting the mouse in my heart.
The stiff whiskers of the mouse
brush down the motes in my soul,
each failure of perfect patience.

Maybe, says my sick mother,
I can die tomorrow.
I would wrap her in long mosses,
I would dip her in salmon water,
I would name myself Rain.
I would be washed clean.

THE GOOD DAUGHTER

When the exorcist came to my house,
I claimed I loved my mother.

Most people think bread is a blessing;
I imagine stuffing it down her gullet.

I imagine lashing her harsh lips
with the stems of yellow glads.

Bless the demons who arrive like peddlers
pushing their cart of indifference.

The word *benign* would constitute
a singular act of charity.

When the exorcist came again,
I announced that my mother was dead.

Once upon a time my fingers were little
and tried to twine in her hair.

HOLES IN THE WORLD

breath from the mouth
blood from the womb

vertebrae of dead whales
reamed by the seas

Lonely,
I studied holes in the world

until a bear took me to wive
and we mated in a cave

Now I tell my bear children,
love these years I am strong

After I turn invisible
all you will find is my spine

I tell my husband the bear,
I am not you

This, I explain, *is the source*
of our lonesomeness

paw to paw
and the air between us

A 58-YEAR-OLD HOMELESS WOMAN LIVED UNDETECTED IN HIS CLOSET

—from a news item

The woman up on my closet shelf lies curled on her side.
Her mattress is narrow and thin. She smells of my soap.

How neatly this stranger stores her small possessions
in a cardboard box with a lid and a string.

I never guessed. It was only how food kept disappearing:
one rice cracker a day, a handful of dried figs, a single

orange from a dozen. But now that our eyes have met,
shall we sit at my table, shall I peel us a second orange?

Or perhaps I'll beg this woman to stay. What a relief
to know at last somebody real inhabits my house.

WHAT DISAPPEARS

Mummified Baby Found Wrapped in Old Newspaper

On my kitchen windowsill: ceramic animals
from too many boxes of Red Rose tea
and a dried pine-knot shaped like a child.

That baby I aborted half a century back
I could have wrapped in the old *Daily News*,
the vanished *Mirror*, the late *Herald Tribune*.

I was far too young to wrap it in my hand-typed
100% cotton rag doctoral dissertation.
What if I had wrapped it in my long yellow hair?

My little grandson fingers my tea figurines:
horse, duck, fish, sheep, turtle, frog.
As far as he knows, I have always been old.

That's fine. I have swallowed so much tea
that the tannin, like magical mummy powder,
has thoroughly dried the skin around my eyes.

THIN PLACES

This, here in my right hand:
one antique screwdriver, burled handle
with brass brads driven through wood
sueded by the touch of my great-aunt.

At ninety-five, her hair dyed red,
she boasted:
>   *I was famous at twenty-five.*
>   *I have always been precocious,*

and then she died—her maiden bones,
a single dried leaf folded shut,
leather pocket, thin coffin of autumn.

Like memory, my hand opening: *thunk*
of her screwdriver hitting the floor.
Let this solidity become my life.

The year we buried my great-aunt,
my daughter was tiny and young—

side by side in the moving car,
we drank milkshakes all the way home,
sucking hard through narrow straws.

LIKE ANY OTHER CHILD

She drinks milk from her two mouths and opens and
shuts all the four eyes at one time.
—a news story from India

Her face is two goldfish in a bowl, two perfect tiny mouths,
four deep and sleepy brown eyes. When the baby smiles,
two suns glow in the sky.

Her eyelashes are the fringed wings of four singing birds
over a single pond. Tiny mirrors glitter in the water
like prayers.

She is her own perpetual double, sacred to her rural village,
a baby Hindu goddess. And the young couple lifting her up
to the TV camera? Solemn, yes, formal,

but quite untroubled. Why must I recall my younger self
tasting hot tears—a stunned and heartsick girl
holding my absolutely normal newborn for photos?

WHY I MUST BUILD A FENCE

Because the skulls of grandmothers
peer into my windows,

because my dog sneaks next door
to chew on the bones,

because the crow on this side
caws at the crow on that side,

because the garden snail curls its shell
in only one direction,

and I can't ever go there.
In my new fence, there will be no gate.

MOTHER OF TWO MISCARRIES AFTER BRIEF PREGNANCY

In that final pregnancy
I breathed lilacs three times

When I breathed lilacs in North Carolina
I was pregnant and didn't know it

I was pregnant in Massachusetts
and knew it among many lilacs

Back in New Jersey I began to bleed
among brown skeletons of lilacs

Now years later at a banquet
a stranger studies my palm

>*you have three beautiful children*
>*and your third is a girl*

So I raise up my wine glass saluting
my lost purple daughter, calling her,

calling her *Lilac, Lilac, Lilac*

HOW TO SURVIVE A FALL THROUGH THE ICE

Always inhabit two climates
Face the direction you came from
Always carry a stout pole

Blindfold all the crocodiles

Think of your maiden great aunt
traveling the world between the wars

Imagine she had an African lover

or else an Eskimo

I like to pronounce *Limpopo River*
Sometimes it almost runs dry
Collect dew by walking at sunrise
with rags tied to your ankles

Did the lover sip dew from her navel

Did he push back her bobbed bangs
to lick fresh ice from her eyelids

When you cover a crocodile's eyes
the crocodile becomes more sedate

The great aunt died with hennaed hair

To escape from a hole in the ice
very, very slowly pull out one
leg at a time

Your aunt never told you this story

Crocodiles often open their mouths
when lightly tapped

A LONG AGO SUMMER WHERE I FIRST EXISTED
AS WHO I WOULD BECOME

In a plane or a dream or the painted cart of the butcher,
how I rode the horizon to my pen pal in the cobbled village
of Cazouls-les-Béziers

where the mayor and the doctor in their black suits
and the one cafe had the only phones in the whole town
and each phone wound with a crank,

and Marie-Claude and I pedaled past vines to the river
and floated in weeds through yellow noon heat,
and when I got sick from too many blackberries,

the crossbar of the borrowed bike
gave me unexpected shivers in my secret crease,
and how, on the night of the great wind,

I glowed with fever and couldn't tell anyone,
not in English, not in French, how waiting wolves
hung on the dark wall by their sharp teeth, those wolves,

les loups sauvages, mon dieu, mon dieu,
much like my faraway parents in that dangerous place
where come September I'd have to go back.

CALLING MY MOTHER AGAIN

I feel so guilty, she repeats, voice thin
and surprised as a child's.

The phone is heavy for her to hold.
I feel so guilty.

    I tell her, *You worked hard all your life.*
    You have no reason to feel guilty.

The white flowers, says my mother.
Always she talks about flowers.

So beautiful the things inside them,
she says. *Long red things.*

Is there anything we can give you
to eat?

    What kind of flowers? I inquire.
    I hear her ask her aide.

And now she reports, *White lilies.*
With red things. I feel so guilty.

The two birds. I don't deserve it.
Everything in this house is beautiful.

Suddenly my ardent mother
is a shining spirit like a mountain

lifting up the entire sky.
It is for this that she has thrashed

her way through life, and now,
in her white cloak of helplessness,

as if from a high place,
she is teaching our poor world

its own magnificence.

OUR JOBS

My mother is busy dying,
my father is turning his bones into dirt,
my children are busy earning enough,
my grandson is painting faces on puppets,
my dog hard at it digging for moles,
my cilantro going to seed.
And what is my business?

I am busy wrinkling,
assiduously chronicling,
way busy laughing
at the busy work of the world:
how a bundle of tiny spiders divides
on this wooden fence post, baby spiders
all so busy going up or going down.

AUTOBIOGRAPHY I: THE PUBLIC LIFE

For much of my life I was so damned ignorant
that I believed in miracles. I didn't believe
in color or clan, I didn't approve
of anger or guns. Old Tom Jefferson
danced a minuet right out of his marble cupola,
tossing cherry blossoms up in the air,
and I sat up and caught them in my baby paws.

I'd been born in our nation's capital.
My child mother clambered up a ladder
to plop me in Abraham Lincoln's stone lap.
That was the year my mother was Black
until I, too blond, blew her cover.
Spring frogs splashed in the Reflecting Pool
over the bent Washington Monument.

I would vote for JFK and wait up for California,
I would weep for him and Bobby and Martin,
I rode Abe Lincoln's slow black locomotive.
I missed the Edmond Pettis Bridge on the March
to Montgomery, I didn't run through flaming Detroit
because I was gathering fallen cherry petals
and stitching them into tiny boats. They capsized.

My mother got old. We had some new wars.
My son had a son. Everything changed. Now
I would make the soldiers deliberately rip
my flesh. I would become a torch
in a liquor store or a gas station. For this boy
I would breathe *Fury, Fury, Fury.*

A STONE WROTE A SONG

A stone skittered downslope to the edge of a river.
The stone sang about summer and fingerling fish.
It sang how the rain raises circles on water.
The stone sang on and on about moss.

When I came through the forest to the same river,
the stone was breathless so I sang for the stone.
I liked being a sister in a duet of stones—
little stone sister, what I have always wanted.

INUIT CAIRN

Help me build a monument
to the man who fed his unmothered child.
He did well.
He was a good father.
Each bedtime he slit a finger
and suckled his child to sleep.
This is a true story.
There are ten fingers
and they all heal.
The child was weaned and grew up
a skillful hunter.

Build the cairn higher
for the woman who hanged her children.
She did well.
She was a good mother.
When she cut down the four little bodies,
they were no longer hungry.
This also is true.
Once she was alone
it was not so bad to starve.
In aftertimes,
when the hunters came back,
she gained much respect.

Let us pile stones
to those who teach us:
the old man with thick fingertips,
the hunter whose childhood is a story,
the old woman cradling a dish.

We must pile many stones
to honor blood:
for the skinned carcass out on the ice,
the gored hunter,
the young girl bleeding
her first time
and frightened
that she might die.

Later this girl will laugh
like oil in a lamp,
like the new water between ice and shore,
like a woman with a man.
She will laugh well
in her brilliant flesh.
This last stone is for her.

HOW MEMORY WORKS

Just as the rose remembers the bud,
likewise the old cookbook enfolds
a red satin ribbon left between pages.

I finger the petal creased in the seam
of my jacket pocket. Even in darkness,
the cookbook cord shines a bloody red.

I mean the rose with black spot mildew,
I mean the cookbook with butter stains.
Memory: that ribbon choking my breath,

one room where the door stays stuck,
the dream where the man on the bus
made me get off at his stop. His stop.

COMMUNICATIONS AT SEA

From the distant beach,
he's finally stopped shouting at me.
I hear only from strangers
who send messages in bottles:

> *Hi, my name is Jimmy.*
> *I live in New Jersey.*

I've floated in this ocean for years now.
Whenever I approach a shoreline,
I let the current sweep me out.

I eat raw fish and open my mouth
to the rain. Ships never see me.

I sleep all day snuggled in weeds
of the Sargasso sea; at night I recite
whatever I like:

> Wordsworth's "Daffodils"
> or the Gettysburg Address.

I keep hoping for a bottle with a pencil.
There's a man I want to write to,
if he's still alive. I want to tell him:

> *When I was with you, I was drowning.*
> *Now I feel safely embraced*
> *when the hurricane howls my name.*

STORIES ABOUT A BROTHER
I NEVER HAD

He is my older brother
No, my younger brother
or else we are twins

We tied our shoes
into one knot
We sipped from this silver cup

Two matched mouths
stretched licorice ropes
from each end

He was my mother-love
He was my pet
He was my second self

After he died
I carried his ashes
by Amtrak

At each station
I chewed a cupful
of silver ash

At the end of the line
I contained my brother,
truest brother ever

MY DEAD MOTHER AS A CALYPSO ORCHID

It pollinates by deception, luring insects it cannot nourish.
The menu at our house was hunger.

Today as I swallow huckleberries along a logging road,
my lips, like the full lip of the Calypso orchid,

are speckled bruise-purple. My mother's eyes sank
into her skull. How blind the word *chide*.

STONE FINGERS

How I have longed to touch them all:

the veined marble fingers of the goddess
in front of her temple, a sacred vapor
arising from the cave,

or up in the central Cascades,
craggy peaks of Three-Fingered Jack:
cloud-shredder, rain-catcher, glacier-shaper,

or blue hands of the newly dead—
how blood will puddle in place, each finger
ready to stiffen, while brow and lips,

such still lips, are still remotely warm,
as if this were a kiss from another world,
the caress that time grants us

after time for caresses has passed.

SMUDGE

Fleets of transparent carriers riding pneumatic wind,
rushing through Macy's, Gimbels, B. Altman's,

hushed whoosh and kerthunk of those bullet-shaped holders
high above wooden floors, over the perfumed waft

of department store air, languorous ladies adrift in their furs,
and my mother's manicured grip like a knife to my wrist,

>and a dark, inexplicable *smudge*
>on my brand new white Mary Janes.

I longed to be small enough to curl into that cylinder, locking
the end behind me, to speed above glass counters, to vanish,

be sucked into some dim inner office crowded with money,
and then to return, changed.

AT SANTIAGO DE ATITLÁN

Crossing over deep water, I found in the wind
my own parents who had come here once
years ago and gone on. All day I had parents.

In the bent reeds of the lake, in the deft fingers
stitching long-tailed birds onto woven blouses,
under awnings of rushes, in a darkened room,

as I knelt in front of Mayan Saint Maximón,
in the mute shamans flanking his body,
in the small flames of my fragile candles,

there my parents became young and joyful
and mine forever, visible and invisible,
like a green parrot in a green tree.

CROW MERCIES

—In memory of Marian Schott,
1919–2009

The Art of the Poetic Line

> High on a wire:
> clothespins or crows

Farewell to the Old Days

> When we were young and beautiful,
> when we were fools

What We Thought Then

> That someone would jump in to save us,
> that you never forget how to ride a bike

Wisdom

> One-who-knew met One-who-didn't-know,
> and it was hard to know the difference

Tyrannies of the Bedspread

> My mother, too old and sick
> to spy it folded up on the chair

Fragility

> The top curve of her left ear
> parting her limp hair

Marriage

> I told my husband,
> *If you die, I'll kill you*

Sexual Dimorphism after Sixty

Long, thick hair in his nose and ears,
sparse or none in her groin

Who Remembers Least?

Humans, crows, ladybugs, ferns, algae,
shoes, toasters, doorsteps, invisible ink?

Jet Set

My mother traveled by air;
now crow flies without her

Party Decorations

When the goldfinches show up,
poppies bobble yellow petals

Botheration

A flock of common grackles conquers
the bird feeder; even crow surrenders

Mercy

Clothespins on socks
or a string on crow's foot

High Fashion

> So like a wood duck, elegant in dress,
> though she spoke with the voice of crow

Ars Poetica

> As a rule, I do not sell my dreams;
> as a rule, I break rules

Flock

> The clothes on the line
> flapped white wings

THE NEXT CHAPTER FROM ANCIENT HISTORY

The barbarians wore sparrows on their bronze helmets
or else it was a trick of the light.

They arrived in a blaze of madness.
The geese at the bridge had neglected to warn us.

Each man sported a garland of cruelty.
They poked sticks into the ashes of our past.

All their accusations were true.
We rattled our seedpods in assent and waited

until our invaders slept. I am hiding inside
this ice cave until their last man

goes home. The one sound in my cave
is the *drip drip drip* of melt.

ON THE MULLICA

The river corners back on itself
like some ancient delta seen from the air,
but this is not the air, only a Grumman canoe
slipping through the shadowed throat where trees touch over water,
where spidery roots slide out of sand,
where red-winged blackbirds flame above cavernous stumps
on the dark banks where nothing holds

until beyond another corner or another or another
until all directions are mixed,
and the river opens out to a shallow meadow of lilies,
its iron water striping the sandy bottom rustbrown and yellow
as the stiff yellow center of each white lily,
and then, from beyond dark cedars at swamp edge,
across tangled weed tufts, comes the last dinosaur,

and though I have no voice to call out to him,
I lift up my paddle like a flag,
but he is too big or too old
or the silver canoe is too bright for him to see me.
He wades upstream among lilies and lilies,
the clear brown ripples dividing around his feet
as if about islands.

BECAUSE THE EARTH IS SLOWING DOWN

the sun sets for longer and longer;
it tints the tree trunks pink.

From a secret cave in the Caucasus
an archer's perfectly crafted arrow

has been flying for centuries. Even
the briefest poppies go on blooming

while the crack in the dry lake bed
stays thinner than one wire plucked

on a balalaika by an old man weeping
because he can't keep time. Consider

the time it takes to grab one grenade
out from the crowded playground,

or how I yanked a mouse by the tail
out of the long mouth of the dog,

off the hot arrow of her tongue—
you won't need to love me any longer

than that.

THE ROUGH-SKINNED NEWT

Did it skitter away from the hissing sticks of our fire?
Did its tail tickle your wet ankle?

Was the flash of its underbelly the color of melon?
Did it disappear under the upside-down rowboat?

Did I tangle my chilled fingers through yours?
Did the rowboat's keel glitter with rain?

Would you wrap me up in your yellow slicker?
Would we follow the newt beneath the boat?

Would we lie there on moss as if it were sheepskin?
Would we speak of the newt as true believers

might converse about ghosts?
.Would I put my lips to the stiff hairs on your neck?

I did. I would.

GREAT EVENTS ABOUT TO BEFALL ME

That was the summer I fell asleep
Poems fell out of the air

I fell crazy in love
I longed to become a fallen woman

When love fell by the wayside
I fell to weeping

Later I fell upon hard times
and fell in with fools

And all this while

on the other side of the continent
they were felling the great trees

PRELUDE

When she was a girl in her mother's kitchen,
she said:

When I'm a grown-up and I have a husband,
I'll also have a potato masher
and a cheese grater
and a garlic press
and some poultry shears.

These she would use
to mash, grind, press, hack apart with shears.

Sweetheart, run do me a favor, said her mother,
rubbing bruised knuckles into reddened eyes.
She handed the girl a list and a ten-dollar bill.

So the girl flounced off in her red skirt
to buy red pepper
and red-leaf lettuce
and Red Rose tea
and a red-hearted Valentine
for Daddy.

To mash, grind, press, and hack apart with shears.

She didn't yet know—her mother hadn't told her—
there could be so much blood
in a marriage.

SUCH HEALING AS THERE BE

Mother, Mother,
I am crackling with thirst.

    Drink, Daughter, drink:
    at dawn a flagon of tarwater,
    cuckoo ale at noon,
    and comet wine by night.

Oh, my mother,
how shall I endure?

    Practice a poultice
    of watercress and spurge,
    catmint and ambergris
    scratched with a pin.

Mother, my mother,
I am burning with love.

    Must I wrap you in henbane?
    Remember, pale daughter,
    when you bed with the Devil,
    his member will be sharp ice.

SWEET EMMA

*—based on picture titles from the Slotin
auction catalog of Southern folk art*

Emma's breasts are two watermelons.
Now she unzips her green dress.

Emma is feeling all goofy and funny
like a smiling fish.

Her little babies in the washtub
play in the water.

The hate snake at the garden gate
won't harm a child of God.

The mighty hand of the Lord,
sometimes it's hard to hold onto.

Her bush is burning.
She thinks God's prick is a cherry tree

blooming with bees. *Uh-huh.*
Sweet Emma gets right with God.

I WILL NOT COUNT THE YEARS
OR EVEN THE HOURS

I will go to the place that stands motionless
inside the middle of a minute.

I will live in that place that tumbles with stars
over the embracing roof of the dark

where I confuse your soft breathing
with wind brushing the Douglas firs.

Long after our moment has ended,
anniversaries of our marriage

could flourish like early salmonberries
by a June trail. I want to believe in love

so bright, so frequent, so delicious,
it ought to be eaten by birds.

TROUSSEAU

Each new bride should know
about men who wait outside.

Assign him his private hut.
Enter as a guest and seldom.

Be sure your questions
concern engines.

Does he want to screw?
Oh, let him.

When he's crabby, don't ask.
If he loses his job, cook.

Remember how much he loves
potatoes—soft yield

of their flesh—though he lives
in terror of inner spaces:

the dark he was born from,
anything that makes him small.

You must learn how to bend
like a willow—sinew and lignin.

Build a room the color of trees
and wrap him in leaves.

THE QUILTER

She lives in a log cabin. Her sunbonnet babies
shriek all day over pinwheels and tumbling blocks.

Each night her man rolls to the far side of the bed.
She slips into boots and opens her garden gate.

She tiptoes past star flowers cut from broken stars.
At the end of a rail fence, she wiggles through

the hole in the barn door. She sits on a hay bale
fingering her own hair. Frayed cotton batting

comes loose in tufts. Moon rise crowds the corn cribs.
A dove in the window calls the time. Enough of this

pieced life. Perhaps it's time to rip off her apron,
lope into the forest, dream a trip around the world

under a bear's claw quilt. She wants to curl deep
into brown fur. She is craving those curved claws.

WHAT WE CAN BE SURE OF

Even as we speak, someone else in the world besides me
is saying, *Even as we speak.*
An average of three children a year are carried away by their kites.
I used to hope that one of them would be me.
When that man went up with balloons and a lawn chair,
I was waiting at 10,000 feet to wave at him.

Someone in the world is killing his neighbor
while someone else is pressing a shirt.
Look: a six-year-old girl is drawing a green dog.
See how she leans to the paper, how she squeezes her crayon,
how the green wrapper is unwrapping from the green crayon.
Imagine a paperwhite narcissus outgrowing its sheath.

Meanwhile the man holds a gun or a machete.
He tries not to see his neighbor's eyes.
Even as we speak, there is so little
we can be sure of. As far as I know,
nobody in Chicago has a pet sea lion,
but please text me if you do.

PICNIC IN THE CLEARING

You think you're safe in this landscape:
the red pond and the blue barn,
incisive beaks of the crows.

You're sure the soldiers will never hunt
you here, that these raw cawings
are echoes of passing flocks.

In the purple shadow of the blue barn,
a graveless man dips leather hands
into the unclotted pond.

Go ahead and eat your sandwich.
None of this is your problem.
But please remember

to leave your crusts. Under lustrous
feathers, the postulant crows
grow hungry.

U.S. AIR FORCE ADMITS IT MAY HAVE BOMBED
CIVILIANS IN AFGHANISTAN

—for my adult children

To lose words, leak urine, gum bread,
to hobble on a stick,

ah, the finest of news. So many years
without gunfire or flame.

Why do you stare, my lively ones?
I call this *good news.*

First I was pretty and then I was dead,
but in between, I got old.

No air force bomber came sprinkling fire
over my wedding.

My babies grew up with both of their hands
and all their skin.

It isn't every day that every mother
gets such great news.

There is a woman whose face is darker
than mine. Her shawl

shadows her eyes. This woman was born
in the wrong village

under the wrong sky. What must we do
to offer her baby

each fresh sunrise like a rich peach
ready for patting

with two plump hands?

BIOPSY

Doctors inscribed my shoulder
with a purple *X*.

They tunneled into my left lung
to translate a spot.

They rummaged behind my clavicle
with their long needle.

> *Breathe in.*
> *Hold your breath.*
> *Breathe out.*

Thus did I diminish my lifetime larder
of air. That night I couldn't shrug.

If a sorcerer has spread seeds
on the altar of my breath,

are they growing? Am I one more
cracked statue, or the dirt clod

clobbered under the great hoof
that draws the plow,

or else an untended field grown-in
with thistle? Meanwhile

my foolish skin doesn't know
we are waiting.

It goes on planning
to shelter me forever.

DEAR LADY,

—for my mother

You, on the couch, becoming a stranger,
do you know who I am?

You hold your newspaper
without reading words.

Your memories are locked in a cupboard
to which neither of us has the key.

When anyone comes to visit,
you smile. You say:

> *My house is so beautiful.*
> *Everybody loves my house.*
> *Dogs like it here.*

If I were a dog, I would curl on the couch
and lean my chin on your thin ribs.

I would lick your bony mother-hand
to show you I am here.

AUTOBIOGRAPHY II: A ROW OF PAINTED DOORS IN THE JUNKYARD

Some with old glass doorknobs
    and layer on layer of peeling paint,
        and all the rooms they led to,
            gone.

Time begins: blue window, black.
    To arrive yelling and sucking,
        shaping mouth to nipple,
            milk blister on the top lip.

Under my grandmother cedar,
    a little girl only imagined
        snails on her shoes,
            air ferns sprouting out of her knees.

To land at the old airport:
    silver propellers slow from blur to blades.
        Where are their waiting faces,
            once so bright at the arrival gate?

Beyond the margins of the long-term lot,
    among cattails and broken bottles,
        an oarless rowboat
            sunk to the gunwales,

while back in the junkyard
    one chipped and battered door
        is swinging wide open
            to where the now familiar *I*,

if not cherished, will be at least,
    at last, invited in.
        Must I pay this world for breath?
        Do fish apologize

for displacing the sea? They will be weighed
    with silver scales.

WELCOME TO BEING DEAD. HOW WAS YOUR TRIP?

How did you fly over?

> By waving good-bye to my roof.
> On the ashen wings of exhaustion.
> Riding a blind wind.

What did you see here first?

> Pink worms.
> The seeds of abandoned snapdragons.
> Holes in the ground.

What had you been expecting?

> Nothing.
> Ancient parents.
> A band of gold-plated tubas.

And what did you settle for instead?

> The silent drip of the Big Dipper.
> The generous swoop of the usher bird
> brushing my head with fringed wings.

IN MEMORY

—Marian Schott,
1919–2009

Tomorrow it will be over
I will fly all night

You will be the beacon
signaling the airplane

I will home in
on your sharp bones

The engines will falter
like your enlarged heart

The plane will land in time
I will drive out of dawn

My sister will be weeping
You will be panting like a fish

Oxygen will grumble and spit
through a hose across the floor

Your crusted tongue will flicker
like the tongue of a snake

The embroidered nightgown
will lie white on blue skin

Let the human vessel
finally be broken

Now I am old and weary
Let me be born

LEARNING THE WORD
T-E-N-D-E-R-N-E-S-S

Picture this:
how after the estate sale
my mother's mink coat
lay tossed in a corner.

Nothing she told me was true.
Nothing she told me was false.
Nothing she told me was kind.
Nothing. She told me nothing.

My first mother was my children.
My next mother was my lover.
My best mother is my white dog:
fur on my skin like sun.

I once had a young mother.
I once had a stylish mother.
I once had a jet-set mother.
I never had a mother.

Now watch how I swaddle
my body in sunlight.
My mouth is a warm "O"
suckling on the alphabet.

THE SHADOW

of the leaf is more engrossing than the leaf:
moment after a kiss, moment before a murder.
Nothing has come of nothing and won't

or hasn't yet. Now I imagine I sent
the president a sonnet and the president
sent me a gun. I would dandle

the gun in my lap like a baby
or a map or a glass basin for augury
or the slimy net I found by the pond.

We are all candle-wasters under the sun.
Whatever a tadpole learns from a frog,
the tadpole is bound to forget.

I think tadpoles think about water
in the same way I thought about time,
testing my fresh feet. I thought

that story plots made sense like a peony
or a symphony or sympathy or the blinking
and perforated shadow

of one leaf of the copper beech,
wide-branched beech tree where I turned
gold-illuminated pages. It was summer,

it was always summer. Only Abe Lincoln
had ever been shot. The sun set late.
My sister and I never got old.

PERFECT TIMING

After I unscrewed the orange top and nibbled white Elmer's glue
because there was a milk cow on the plastic bottle,

after I came home from eighth grade with all *A*'s and an *A+*,
because *A-* meant *less-than-Adequate*,

after I lost my cherry and got knocked up first time out
because I didn't know how to say no,

after I got a psychiatrically approved legal abortion
because my well-connected parents pulled fancy strings,

after I hurried up and married a grump to produce a child
because the abortionist had said *Abortion can leave you sterile*,

after I almost suffocated my first baby
because I knew that I couldn't kill myself and leave him motherless,

after the grump dumped me and I rushed sleepless through my thesis
because I needed a tenure-track job to feed my kids,

after the doctors stapled my throat in a ring
because they had slit it to cut out the cancer,

after I swam and swam and kept counting my strokes
because I knew no other prayer,

I finally abandoned striving
because I had stopped expecting *Ever After*,

whereupon I found how easy this life became:
the fishes scooting through grasses under the reflective face of the pond,

and now, just past twilight, as I saunter into the pond, my toes rippling
the wet stars.

AUTOBIOGRAPHY III: MY DISENCHANTED LIFE

Among commercial elves and sad trolls parked
under bridges, I'm a highway fairy princess.
I drive high in the cab of my rig, cruising
the interstate fifteen miles over the speed limit,
radar turned on. When my eyelashes tremble,
I pull into truck stops and park at the edge
to spoon nectar out of lupines and sip dewdrops
from foxgloves. I tell you I've chosen this life.

But this princess dreams no enchantment, only
a stacked trailer of crated chickens clucking
like tunes from an unstrung lute. I try to
re-string the lute with spider silk. Its dry frame
buckles. I try to re-glue it with cobwebs.
Nothing works: my GPS unit can't get a signal,
jumper cables are no damn use. I switch on
my CB radio: *Hopeless Princess / over and out.*

Once a month I repeat this route. Usually
to the music of chickens, I pick up a new man
who's no damn prince. Such a long haul back
to the lush meadow beyond the lot. Each trip,
I toss a bloody blanket out of my truck.

RECLINING NUDE

1. Service

I opened my eyes and stopped counting.

His breaths quickened.
He made small groaning sounds back in his throat.
The flat of his belly quivered and lay still on top of me.

His body was sour with sweat and felt too heavy,
and the angle at which he had finished
pulled at my pubic hair.

He trembled once more and breathed out *Thank you.*

I could have been anyone performing a necessary service.
It was as if I had brought him a cup of coffee

or, better, a cold beer.
I could have been no one.

2. Why I Don't Want to Sleep with Michelangelo's *David*

The large stiff fingers
and well-carved pubes

his rippled abs
the polished thighs

cradled in muscles
harder than marble

I have lain over years
with the same man

on nights when the body
says *yes*, says *now*

Perfection never his name
no marble curls

but the glue of bellies
soft mammalian hair

chest pressing chest
legs wrapping legs

the rumpled bed of morning
the tolerant dog

3. What I Am

I want to lock all my diplomas
inside a dark closet

I want to drive to a honky-tonk
in my battered red truck

I want to pick out a man
just for his hat

I want his faded jeans
to hang from his hips

I want his grammar
to be non-standard

and his breath
sweetened with brandy

When he asks me my name
I'll tell him *Sally*

and he'll never guess
how Yeats runs in my head

> *Down by the salley gardens*
> *my love and I did meet*
> *She passed the salley gardens*
> *with little snow-white feet*

I want him to walk me
back to my truck

and push me hard
up against the tailgate

where I stand on tiptoe
in my red boots

I want him to think
he knows who I am

4. Photo: Reclining Nude

How her beauty
was once my beauty:

her raised hip as landscape,
the shadowed line of the spine,

how the tongue of my eye
journeys the long plain of the back,

how my five right fingertips
tremble to sculpt her grainy flesh,

how her hip and my hip
bask in the glance of the lens

5. *Winter Is Long, Our Beauty Is Gone*

The dream ran on and ran again,
the body rehearsing its decay.

All last night our loose bed sheet
made a white meadow.

I stepped over wrinkled snow
wheeling my wooden barrow

through sheds of the dead.
Staccato breaths gurgled

and caught in your throat.
At first pinkness of dawn

your rough square fingertips
brushed across my face.

You claimed you loved me,
and I had to sit up and laugh.

Just look at us: two old people,
their eyes masked by light.

THERE ONCE WAS A HORSE WHO LOVED HIS BELLS

The dark cortège of carriages clatters to the dump,
dashing forth to hold cold court among rats and rot.

From which cruel window will a curtained face
curse the little cart horse as he canters the cobbled lane?

But the dear little horse just lifts his hoof and twitches
his coarse hairiness. Hear his bells ring. Nothing,

not even the bare brassiness of his unpolished buckles,
the ochre brown of blindered eyes, can ever disguise

his own mute gladness.

THE GOODNESS OF MY HEART

—for my first husband,
father of my children

I forgive you over and over.
I forgive you for being so selfish.
I forgive you for lording it over me.
I even forgive you for mocking me
in the presence of our small children.

I forgive you weekends and Christmas,
the worst day of all. I also forgive you
the times I pounded my own forehead
hard against the car window
because you'd twist what I'd just said.

I forgive you when azure skies lift me
and great trees float backwards, almost
falling over. Yes, it's getting easier
to forgive you, but you never manage
to stay forgiven, so I forgive you again

no matter how long you've been dead.

BLOSSOM AND DIMINUENDO

I hid my first bloody panties under the bed
where a bad smell led my mother to discover
what I hadn't been willing to tell. Our drive
to Walgreens made a pale ritual. *Always,*
she said, *use cold water to wash out blood.*

When you cross-stitch flowers on dishtowels
without a thimble, the towel often blossoms
bright red. I wanted a wedding and kitchen
and babies, and what I got was roses, roses.

My mother's brother died in World War II.
Last year she could say, *I love my brother,*
present tense. Now she never had a brother.

I know no way to prettify this story. My eyes
are stained with blood. Sticky green liquid

from a cut daffodil cruds up my camera lens.

MEMORIAL

On stained asphalt
in front of the Union Gospel Thriftshop,
a weathered old guy is busy rounding up
stray shopping carts.

The overhang of his belly
half conceals his wide silver belt buckle.
One battered cart has yellow nylon twine
snagged in a front wheel.

The cart refuses to be corralled.
Up on the curb, an abandoned radio blares
its symphony. The wild violins outdistance
the cellos—drums, like horses,

galloping away.
He herds metal carts into other metal carts.
Each cart clangs like a chuck wagon gong.
Across the street, late sun

glints orange off gas station glass.
But now the man lingers. He lingers.
He has always been useful. He stumbles.
Why do I tell his story?

In lieu of flowers.

DROWNING BECOMES ME

The fox announces the separateness of others.
She is delicate in her navigations past secret hollows
behind the dunes.

I used to rub my hands over your skin.
Now the grasses blow sideways.
Fickle and feckless, a bird in the beach-plum whistles.

When I think how I loved you, I know
I would still stomp into the deepest gulches of the waves
just to catch your floating hat.

IN PRAISE OF WORK

Today I will praise the sacred names
of work: *to scrub, to weave, to cook,*
to do and do, order entire battalions,
harvest honey from inside the hive.
Today I will do all the jobs in the world.

What work so urgent as that of a thorn
or a lumpy purple-and-yellow piñata?
Thorns and piñatas, pain and delight,
those twin sisters who pulled me out
of my mother, the hardest work of all.

THE LESSON

The party dresses of mothers
wilt like silk flowers.

The mothers were fairy princesses;
they have all danced away.

Now we are older than our mothers
and our cheeks are softer than talc.

We will never be beautiful enough
to deserve ourselves.

The wings on our party shoes
gash the flesh of our heels.

Our steps leave a blood trail
our daughters will follow.

THE GEOLOGY OF MY GRANDPARENTS' HOUSE

A volcano in that house of small tremors,
a hot rock of disappointment

    Magma may be drained from the chamber
    through fissures at depth

Here is my grandfather, handsome young businessman,
good catch, and my grandmother posed
in her pale blue engagement dress,
skirt and bodice encrusted with seed-pearls

    Essential in plains is horizontal layering
    without notable crustal disturbance

until their first daughter dies of a fever,
and my grandfather loses his hair and his money,
and the only son dies in the war,
his death the measure of every grief,
and my grandfather mows the lawn in his bathrobe

    Lacustrine or lake plains are sediment-
    covered bottoms of lakes gone dry

while my sad grandmother keeps dusting
her father's ruby brandy decanter

    Buried terrain:

how Granddaddy walks my sister and me
to that slight bump called Indian Hill,
how he tips the hat on his bald head,
how he buys us each double scoops
that mound up in our cones like frozen
igneous hills, like lava grown cold

MILLINERY

The human skull is like our planet's mantle,
composed of separate plates. Just fold back
my scalp and you'll see where edges meet.

If there's a soul or anything to make me *me*,
I think it must tremble under those knit bones.
No wonder we live in a world topped with hats:

motorcycle helmets splashed with stars,
the furled jester's cap hung with silver bells,
the artist's black beret with its woolen nipple.

Under this hat, my fragile skull feels crammed
with all I remember: light falling from a porch,
the sick crunch of metal at the bad intersection,

or being small enough to rest a sleepy cheek
on the dog's shoulder and being almost sure
the dog will speak to me in words I understand.

At last I know what any wise dog would say:
Eat what you get. If it's bad, throw up. Bark
until somebody listens. Sleep with the pack.

Dig deep. It's nice to put your head in a hole.
Wet earth smells delicious. Wherever
you can reach, scratch. Remember to wag.

Okay, I smile, nodding my itchy soul.
But how do you like my lime-velvet cloche?

CHILD IN DIMESTORE BLISS

I called it *Wellworth*, gladly offering forth
my warmed-up nickels, coins of opulence,
to this, the first glimpse of Loving Abundance.

I worshipped the visible logic of aisles,
prismatic racks of cotton thread all "mercerized"
on wooden spools to string as necklace beads

for giants.
Woolworths, McCrory's, the *Ben Franklin Five and Dime.*

In *Lampston's* basement, flocks of parakeets:
green, yellow, blue. Where else on this blue earth
flew thus much blue? Turquoise, azure, aquamarine.

    Oh, grant me this day
    the full counter of Abundance:
    whatever, for once, I want,

    from any Five and Ten,
    or wanted then.

ALL THE GRIEF IN THE WORLD

Bird thoughts lift me, reckless
above meadows. I turn pilgrim

in the monastery of air:
gravity as the converse of prayer.

In late sunlight the silver torsos of jets
reflect my ascensions.

Below, my cousins the great whales
roll their rubbery skins.

Fishy breaths from their blowholes
mingle with sorrow's wind

as it spins off the tips of my wings.
I think I am far from home

until, netted around me,
the magnetic field of the earth

chimes in my brain,
I am your roof and your bed.

ENCOUNTER IN VINDIJA CAVE,
PRESENT-DAY CROATIA, LATE OCTOBER

Slowly the woman stepped toward me,
rope sandals wrapping her feet.
Behind her, in a leather bucket
hung from a stick, something boiled.

I had walked backward for 38,000 years.
We met at the mouth of her cave.
Wind swooped up from the valley
and a lizard skittered over sunlit rock.

Tangles of red curls embraced
the broad planes of freckled cheeks.
She puckered her lips before she smiled.
She raised thick brows to beckon me in.

How long had my species been lonely?
We had traveled through ice and floods
until I found her here in an older world.
I knelt to her wildness. One fingertip

dabbed at my forehead. I tried to meet
her green eyes. They seemed too far apart,
averted or appraising, like a seamstress
or an untamed beast. She stroked

my woven blouse, pressed stained palms
to my breasts. Big knuckles lifted my chin.
A moment: we opened our mouths and sang
in a language neither of us knew we knew.

Together in her cave the two of us ululated.
We keened, we psalmed, we spoke *woman*
and silence. It was cold October, old October,
and we curled together on straw.

FUGITIVE MEMORY

In that old language nobody speaks,
a river is rolling its storehouse of stones;

over and over, the river repeats
its own real name, oldest word on the map.

I watch a stranger step out from birchwood
with twin crows riding his shoulders;

from deep in an ice cave under a boulder,
a tall woman and her dog crawl out like a mist.

Now they call to me from across the river
and from so far back, I can never cross over.

In an old language nobody speaks,
how will I talk to my gods?

INVENTION

As the mussel adheres to its wet rock,
as my widowed neighbor scours her house,
as a lizard's tail can shift a tall dune,

so this is the song of one word: *love*;
this is the song of two words: *you, me*;
this is the song of three words: *all of us*—

infinitesimal creatures unknown in the sea;
each star, including new ones so far away
we haven't yet seen them; the invention

of words; wind creasing our fur, or the fur
of whoever we'll be next.

IN THE HOLLOW UNDER THE WET LEAF
DWELLS A FLOWER WITH YELLOW STAMENS

If I ever die, our mother used to announce, *If ever*, from the center
of her own world, and then I forget what she said next, just
her permanent certainty against mortality.

Weather blows in, or a brown bird with pin eyes, or one slim finger
of the east wind, or whatever begins and lingers and changes
the small space beneath the rain-wet leaf.

The last surprise will be dying. My finger caresses our mother's
hand, pressing her thin skin, she who was minister of knuckles,
admiral of blue veins, secretary of delicacy, grand pooh-bah

of the great *Ah-ha*. How the span between her thumb and forefinger
is a frog's throat, how that almost transparent membrane moves out
and in, trying to swallow sky,

how I once saved a frightened spider with a 3x5 card and carried it
out to the yard, how we hope Fate won't squish us. If names exist
where our mother is going,

I won't call her *Mommy*, or *Old Lady*, or *Neglected Third Daughter*,
child who leaped off her front steps shouting her name to the whole
unlistening street: *I am Marian-The-Great*.

Meanwhile the bird, that completely unidentifiable pin-eyed bird
whose down trembles at an old woman's sparse breath, that small
brown bird, requires no name.

If I ever die, said our mother, said our mother, more than once.
Now her words diminish along with her flesh. Tonight I would like
to slip her emaciated body onto a white card

and carry her to safety under a wet leaf. Perhaps at the end
we ought to address her as *Marian-If-I-Ever-Die* which sounds like
the name of a rare wildflower.

The country inside the flower owns no speech, but pollen knows
each language in perfect silence. Over a parchment forehead,
as her eyes sink,

may stamens sprinkle yellow absolutions.

CASING THE TERRITORY

North of Maupin in the gap
between hills, you see it all—

glacial slope of Mount Hood
where rock-silt water collects,

down to the railroad trestle
where the White River spills

into the rushing Deschutes,
the whole course of a river

in one glance. Like knowing
from the moment I was born

where I'd tumble past rapids
and how I am meant to die.

I WANT YOU TO BELIEVE THIS:

Somewhere on this planet you have a precious sister
you don't know.

She escaped from your parents' house before she was born,
but she has always watched you.

Whenever you cross a bridge, she holds up the fragile air
beneath you.

Once as you shoveled snow, you glimpsed her in the ice fringes
of your own hair,

or you mistook her for a lone dawn coyote, not understanding
the frisson of love between you.

Whatever your affliction, she arrives across water to help you
carry your halo of pain.

After she has vanished like mist over an estuary, you know
you will survive.

Believe this: now that your unseen sister has come to caress
your eyelids, you may trust

the double abutments of every bridge, you may stop apologizing
for your life.

SLEEP AS A MEADOW

See how the sky sails by,
over hedgerows and stiles.

Go to bed. Tonight
you can be like my child.

Let your eyelids yield to the dark
though they enfold fields.

Even the fleecy sheep
graze easy up on the hill,

their tongues an unguent
to dreams. Sleep. Sleep.

Call this my lullaby: all night
for the both of us

I'll be tending those fires
that ignite the stars.

FUN TONIGHT! A COMPOSITION IN EIGHTEEN FRAGMENTS

1. The Cry of the Eagle

Have you heard it, that small pipping,
that high *meep*? Wingspan

of disbelief.

2. Claim

This is not a poem.
It doesn't rhyme
or make you cry.

But you're reading it,
sailor. Something
might just turn up.

3. Go sail the world

only to arrive
in the brown eyes of the harbor seal.

4. Bringing in the Nets

He brought back the sea on his skin,
its silver flakes.

For years I believed I loved him.
What I loved was the sea.

5. A Dream I Intend to Dream

White cathedral with white arches,
white dresses by a blue boat.

6. In the Collapsed Barn

Ghost brides tethered to rings,
ghost horses mouthing gray hay.

7. Work

We used to believe
in wheels and smokestacks.

Now we forget
the high ridge of the biceps,
the tendons of the neck.

8. By the Canal

Stooped, hair white in their ears,
old men recall the swimming hole.

They don't speak of their own beauty,
their slick, straight backs.

9. Urgent Request

To this village of saucers and butter knives
and sweetly folded sheets, please send
wolves. I miss my brothers.

10. Cougar

Crouched high among rocks,
the cat surveys.

You, walking the narrow defile,
do not forget the word *prey*.

11. Query

Naked design
of the white skull—

what use,
the top hat and cane?

12. Burial

Is there any sound in the world
like dirt hitting wood?

13. *Fun Tonight! Fun Tonight!*

Shiny bottles,
fine new shoes,

full moon
over the alley,

and nothing, sister,
nothing to lose.

14. At the Theater

That woman in row three
who yelled out to Othello,
Watch out, he's lying—

the play is for her.

15. Big Decision

All day I have wondered what to do with my wrists:
slit them with a bread knife or check my pulse?

Neither, my sweet. Instead, I shall ride downtown
in a golden coach and flaunt my silver bracelets.

16. Although we will die,

each Sunday morning you spend
a precious half hour reading the comics

and giggling out loud, and summoning me,
comic strip by comic strip, to come take a look,

and I come running.

17. Three words

are enough: *Come to me.*
The owl who dwells under cedar
has fewer.

18. Prayer

Meadow of bear grass with your white plumes,
wave for me;

meadow of lupine with your blue undulations,
be my last sky.

THE SARAH LANTZ MEMORIAL POETRY BOOK PRIZE

This poetry book prize was established when Eleanor Wilner and Robert Weinberg gave a generous donation to commemorate the work of Sarah Lantz, whose first book, *Far Beyond Triage,* was published by CALYX Books in 2007. Soon after her husband returned from Iraq in 2006, Sarah Lantz collapsed with a brain tumor. The surgery extracting the tumor affected the area of her brain controlling language and left Sarah with aphasia. As her first poetry book moved toward publication, Sarah could no longer rely on her remarkable language skills or her memory during the editorial process. With great patience and defiant humor, Sarah worked on the manuscript with CALYX editors. While we hoped she would live to see the final copy of this book, Sarah reassured us of her delight as she held the galley in July 2007. She knew her time was running out. She died on September 10, 2007, the month before *Far Beyond Triage* was released. This prize stands as a memorial to a great poet, writer, thinker, and enthusiast for life.

ABOUT THE AUTHOR

Penelope Scambly Schott has published three poetry narratives, four poetry collections, and five chapbooks, including *Six Lips* (2010). She has received a Hopwood Award, a Lannan Foundation Fellowship, a Poetry Society of America prize, and four fellowships from the New Jersey Council for the Arts. *A Is for Anne: Mistress Hutchison Disturbs the Commonwealth* received the 2008 Oregon Book Award for Poetry. She has a PhD in late Medieval English literature from City University of New York.

COLOPHON

Titles are set in Tempus Sans ITC.
Poem text is set in Futura Light.

Typesetting and layout by
ImPrint Services
Corvallis, Oregon